little astronaut

little astronaut

J. Hope Stein

Andrews McMeel
PUBLISHING®

little astronaut

prologue: maternity pants

Maternity Pants

I always look a little pregnant
        but this is ridiculous.
One part titty-porn/One part maternity pants.
I have the libido and appetite of a college freshman—
        Hormone-soup & sleepless.
I misread the word MEGA-DROUGHT as MEGA-DOUGHNUT.
I am a hotdog-eating vegetarian
and when I sex, the contractions go on for days.
I can feel my belly grow when I walk
        into a home improvement store.
I am the silly result of blood flow—
        When it flows to my nipples, I am nipples.
        When it flows to my uterus
        I am a poem.

little astronaut

little astronaut

a newborn rests her head on the earth of mother.
everything else is outer space.

An orbit doesn't have a bed

I wander back and forth from the bed of a baby to the bed of a husband. By the time I get to the husband's bed, my shirt is still off, my nipples still wet and pointed and wanting to be touched by anyone but a baby when he puts them in his mouth.

When we are done, I sleep with the baby.

sunrise

the parenthesis
of newborn lips
about to open
(. . .

A toast to the third arm

To the stranger who offers to hold a door for me—
No need, I walk backwards into doors to inspire
a third arm.

To strangers who hand me napkins,
I guess I look like I could use a napkin.

To the stranger yelling across restaurant tables—
HOW'S THE BABY SLEEPING?
—She doesn't—
I play her whale songs all night to aid her infant sleep.

I carry the feeling of being underwater
around with me
on a sunny July Morning.

To the two strangers who scold me—
where's the baby's sunhat!
—as I walk down my own street—

I am Johannes Kepler
tracking the angle of sun
using the planet of my body
to shade her.

To the stranger who follows me down the street
as I hold an 18-pound car seat,
a 10-pound diaper bag
and an 8-pound baby—

            then heckles me
as I decline his help—
You women want to do everything yourself!—

He comes closer— I decline his help again.
He comes closer. I decline—
You women want to do everything yourself—

He is too close to the cab—
I accidentally hit my daughter's tiny head into a cab door.
The baby is screaming.
I am holding her. I am tangled up
in an 18-pound car seat and 10-pound diaper bag—

He is almost in the cab—
I don't have a hand to close the door—
He comes closer and I
–FFFV–
He is almost in the—and I—
FFFHUDHUDHUD—
FFFFVVVFVDFVDFVDVUUDHDHDRVRHUH—
That's "get the fuck away from my baby"
in whale song.
And I slam the cab door.

To the guy drinking on an East Village street-corner
chanting *God bless the baby* as I pass—
Thanks, guy.

To my dear, neglected husband—
he would like to go on a date with me,
last night was kind of rough, luv—

To get this look: sleep deprivation and spit up in the hair.

lullaby

little-milk-breath of
morning,
you sip me as day-bread.

you give me no milk-break
milk-drunk of wee-hour,

you little
mustache.

little-milk-mouth of cloud-break you suck in the dusk-hour,
you suction the turtle-tide,

little milk-shake of lunch-hour, you little mustache.
you yawn.
dawn.
yawn into milk.

A Toast to the Crooked Nipple

To my nipple—a crooked straw
from her drinking like this—

To bathtubs of tepid and shallow waters—
When she is with fever,
I don't need a thermometer
to tell her temperature,
we are always touching.

To the oversized towel
I wrap us in so we look like one person—
and to the mirror
in which we look like one person.

We pay for sex

We agree that the sex is better when we pay for it. That we are getting away with something while living under the oppression of a little tyrant. We pay Anna Norman from my yoga class 20 US dollars to hold our baby in another room while we have sex.

I remind him be gentle . . . I remind him be slow . . . with the pregnancy, birth, and breastfeeding everything is tender and somehow new.

Your ass, he says . . . I'll give him that.
I do a strengthening workout so I can be a stronger mother.

Gentle, they're sensitive.
I remind him the milk is for her . . .

By the end, neither of us is gentle.
He tells me I'm an angel . . . I put my shirt back on while he is still inside me . . . time is money.

Before you were born there were cats

& when the cats died of old age
your father's eyes gathered light
& grew feline in the wink–
He grew me a beard for fuzz to pet
& I said, "Hey, Beard-o!
I missed you while we were sleeping."

Dear Oona, If in a conversation with your significant other about the future—

Believe them if they say they don't want to take care of a baby. If in a conversation about the future, you respond by saying that you have no intention of changing your life, wait to meet your child before you laugh at other parents while promising to be nothing like them. Saying, *it's not good for the kid or the parent to act that way.* Before your child is born, you might say things like, *It's the baby who will have to learn to integrate into my life not the other way around.* Next thing you know you are walking down the street, your baby in a stroller crying, her father trying to talk to you about his day and you stop him to say, *She doesn't like it when we talk—* and you walk ten blocks in silence. Wait, you could find yourself alone in a hospital bed in the middle of the night, the father away on business because you insisted nothing change once the baby is born—and you, at the hospital in the middle of the night, unslept, on painkillers—but holy shit the pain— unable to stand, your baby one day old, left in a bassinet across the room by nurses saying she is inconsolable in the nursery, you cannot stand, she cries out, you stand, you sway you sing you feed, no matter your fresh stitches, she stops crying when you hold her, holy shit the pain, you do not let her go until morning, you wait it happens in a moment.

Prank Calls from Fish

The first time your father kissed me my cell phone fell out of my pocket into the Hudson River and to this day I still receive prank calls from fish.

When astronauts look at earth from space

When astronauts look at earth from space,
they don't see borders.
They don't see the flag-flown territories of So-and-So.
No cattle no stockpile no checkpoint.

They see life on earth from the cockpit
of ayahuasca or mescaline or peyote
or whatever vehicle it is
that allows one to see—

Five—four—three—two—one—
I lift my daughter over my head—

Even this linguini
of drool
that noodles
its way from the interstellar of her mouth
to my nose-tip
(never been kissed like this)
is a connection.

Accessory

In our country—
the bullet of the nipple,
which nourishes you,

must be concealed in the chamber
of a blouse.

But I can if I want to
wear a small gun, cocked

like a shiny
extra finger

or pin it ornamental
to my bust.

A Toast to the Car Seat on My Bathroom Floor

To the car seat on my bathroom floor—
this is how I take my showers—
itsy-bitsy-peek-a-boo with one foot in the air
and the curtain half-drawn—
If the bathroom starts to fly away the baby is secure!

To the backflip she does off the bed—
I move like a character
from *Crouching Tiger, Hidden Dragon*
to catch her—

Stick my fingers
in her toothless mouth
—Pull out a piece of poop—

No idea how it got there—
Her? —The cat?
—No idea whose poop.

To the scar shaped like a smile
at my vaginal hairline
where they pulled her from me—
And the moon-sliver
She claws from my cheek-flesh
when I try to put her in a crib—
The girl WILL NOT SLEEP IN A CRIB—

To my poor husband,
he would like to go on a date with me,
sorry, luv, I'm exhausted—

I hold her all night and the scar that is a smile speaks
to the scar that is a moon.

A Toast to the Dark Side of Earth

To the International Space Station, circling earth
once every 93-minutes,
which is exactly how long
my daughter sleeps.

To the pyrotechnics of fireflies, luminous as cities.
That's what astronauts see on the dark side of earth.
Humans shimmering like stars.

A Toast to the Finger

To my daughter—you are the finger
that causes the finger
to switch on the lamp.

Lullaby for Lamplighter

There are many days
inside each night (*morning,*
little lamplighter,
little lamplighter)
and what dots my sky
is your punctuality
and (*morning, again*
little lamplighter,
little lamplighter)
your punctuation.

A toast to something beautiful flapping in the wind

To something beautiful flapping in the wind above the
beach houses—A blue bird?—No, a blue bag.

To her breath— raindrops in the begonia bed.
My eyesight is rainstorms.

      Drop,

                drop—

To 4 a.m., her first ocean—
Everyone is sleeping
except Oona and the ocean,
Oona and the ocean.

I try to explain in whale song I try to explain in
cloud and water droplet.

      Drop,

drop—

Spending time with a baby is spending time with something
that has lived her entire life in an ocean and just sprouted
legs for land—

I am Copernicus using the planet of my body
to umbrella the wind
as she feeds—Ouch!—

I stick my fingers in her mouth
and she's grown sharp little fish teeth—

Drop,

Everyone is sleeping except Oona and the ocean,
Oona and the ocean
and the little fish teeth.

Drop,

drop,

drop

drop,

I tell time by counting teeth-marks around the crooked
nipple.

The Nod

She wipes sand off my nipple
and drinks
but there's sand
on the hand she wipes with.

Do you like it when I pour sand on your feet?
Something shakes itself silly.
The affirmation of the head.

     A gesture
that brings along with it
the radishing
rubbery nipple.

voyager

An Infant Reaches

An infant reaches for something—I don't know what—pushes it farther away and cries in frustration each time she reaches, not realizing she is crawling for the first time.

She is like her father.

Voyager 2 & Voyager 1

Sometimes my husband
leaves bed
for a little spacewalk
and ends up with a case of aliens
in his throat.

When I try to wake him
it's as though I've punctured a hole
in the oxygen tank
of his reality
and for a few moments he is just gasping,
a visitor here.

Hello luv, we live on earth.

From the outer rims
of our solar system, earth
just looks like a pixel of
blue light caught in a sunbeam.
Not even a pixel—

That's what Voyager 2 & Voyager 1
saw from the edge of our heliosphere
And that's the way my husband looks at me
when I wake him—

Like our life here on earth
is a half-pixel deep
and hardly to be believed—

Earth, luv, we live on earth.

My husband moves like an earthworm
across the carpet.
Does his best monkey.
Motions as if to offer a string
connected to something in sky
& I take it.
We act as two animals holding invisible balloons.

a balloon

the number I balloon
tied to the banister
outside our front door
with a piece of string
looks like a golden
boner

The Now-Clock

The now-clock is the clock of a toddler in which every
number is replaced by the word "now" and the hands
of now are always pointed directly at the now or
between two nows.

Song of the Slip-Prone

little-foot-soles
wobble-
wobble-thump—
little enthusiasms—*wobble-wobble*,
the acquaintance of
new feet.

a puddle

a toddler dances naked in the window
with a gob of summer squash in her hair
then slips in a puddle of her own urine

(seeing her dad pee)

careful daddy!
don't drop your penis in the toilet.

a trashcan

a toddler topples
a trashcan
like a raccoon.

I'm not going to stop her,
or the raccoon.

We have so much garbage—
in this house,
in this country—
on this planet.

Dear Oona, what if human beings
are just diurnal
furless raccoons?

The Dishes

In our house there is always a congregation of ants summiting around a noodle or carrying their weight in popcorn across the kitchen floor. And in the sink there is always a pile of dishes. But this morning your father did something that really made me want to fuck him.

He did the dishes.

Dear Oona, at this moment *Johann Sebastian Bach*, *Chuck Berry,* and *barking dogs* are all on a golden record with a phonograph and intergalactic instructions traveling outside our solar system toward an encounter.—First came song, then came the vessels to carry. *River-song, leaf-song, songs of The Aborigine*—all aboard Voyager 2 & Voyager 1 traveling through space at 31,490 miles-per-minute, which reminds me of your father when he walks down the street. *Frog song, kissing song, coo of mother and child*—It is a songful, songful planet. A planet drenched in song. A circulatory system for song—Dear Oona, *Windsong, Louis Armstrong, night-chant of the Navajo*—what if we are all just space probes looking for water, looking for life? What if we are all just space probes filled with song?

Lullaby for Voyager

Voyager 2 & Voyager 1
are filled up with our song, luv
Voyager 2 & Voyager 1
are gonna outlast the sun, luv
Voyager 2 & Voyager 1
are filled up with our song, luv
Voyager 2 & Voyager 1 . . .
but I'll keep singing to you, luv

We Learn to Dance

My husband, I think he misses me.
I think this because he told me.
I hear him saying this.
I hear him saying I said it wouldn't be like this.
I hear myself saying, sorry, luv, I—

Sometimes you don't know what you need.
Sometimes you know but you don't know how to ask.

All the talking we do—and the writing—
especially the writing—
is so far from what we are meant to be doing—
which I am now convinced is dancing—

She learns to dance before she learns to speak—
and when she hears a song she recognizes
she waves hello—

We fan the air in front of our faces to say she took a shit
or to say a certain dictator stinks like maggots.

But right now, my husband is playing guitar
and singing something real stupid—
Itsy-bitsy peek-a-boo
and songs about babies who won't sleep—

The three of us twirling like idiots—
We learn to dance before we learn to speak.

A Songful Planet

little-palms *slap*
my husband's belly *bango-*

bango (&
pipsqueak giggles)

bango-bango-drum

confetti

(a little finger brushes a piece of hair behind my ear):

What made us, mommy?
I remember me making you
make yourself.

The Director

In the summer of the thrice-broken-toilet,
a fallen shutter, and two positive pregnancy tests,
the cat was in heat
& I was dumber than an embryo.

That there was blood in the ocean
was unimportant.
I saw her face through the water
& threw bread & the fish ate it.

These embryos, they may as well be geniuses
the way they burrow in
and invent themselves a home.
A four-chambered heart,
two halves of a brain and two body-purifying kidneys.
It reminds me of how smart
I used to be.

In the first week of the 2nd pregnancy,
the cat was humping me in my sleep
and I dreamed you moved your hand over me like this
and when I woke I told you I dreamed your hand
moved over me just like this
and I moved your hand just like this just like
I am doing right now.

That there was blood in the water
was unimportant.
I threw bread & a shark
made like a flame and ate it.

These embryos,
the way they hold on
and let go.

In the second month of the 1st pregnancy
I dreamed a celebrated director
cast you as a likable father
with a wife and a son
and another little one on the way.
And that's when I told you—

The first pregnancy of the summer is over.
But this director, he sees you as I do.
As a father.

And your hand
moved over me just like this
just like I am doing
right now.

Before you were born, a magic trick

I bled and bled. I thought of friends who have gone through much worse and I bled. I thought of women across the world and in our own country who have no medical care and bled. I thought of blood and its magic trick—flowing cell-by-cell through time without ever leaving the body. How differently it performs than other liquids—

> girl, I whisper
> to my belly,
> before they told me you are a girl,

> my body may fail you,
> (sorry),

> but know this: your life belongs to you
> & our time together

> it has already begun.

morning, mommy.

I can't get out of bed.

I can help you!
(*waves magic wand*)
Wish-magic—get out of bed!

Because I cannot let her magic not work
I am up—
Or because her magic works.

Dancing, before you were born

It was like the universal scene
for miscarriage
in the language of film
when I woke up in a pool of blood.

The doctor said the trouble
was with my placenta.
—"But right now, the baby's dancing."

Right now, the baby's dancing.

checklist

At 8 weeks it's arm-buds.
11 is teeth-buds.
At 20 weeks it's the eggs of my grandchildren.

But I was monitoring organs—
How many weeks until—If my body gave out—
She could survive?

At 12 weeks the kidneys
begin their lifelong passion
to excrete urine. Check.

At 25 weeks—the brain required for consciousness
(check).

At 40 weeks the lungs breathe a sigh of relief.
At 40 weeks she must leave me
to come to me.

Confetti

I wake to a town populated by fairies and sea creatures and dinosaurs, and my daughter is brushing her hair with a seashell—Several fairy offerings lay on my pillow—a teacup, a mushroom, a drawing of the sky—there are monkeys and glitter in the sky—And I am decorated—with orca whales and narwhals and homemade confetti—which slide off me when I stretch or fidget. And all the dolls of the room are cared for—lined up and tucked under a blanket—*shhh*—*all my babies are sleeping.*

morning, mommy.

I can't get out of bed.

I will help you.
(*pulls hand as hard as she can
putting all her weight into it*)

      I am up—
Because I can't let her strength not lift me
or because she is strong.

A Toast to the Small Gash

To my doctor casually asking: thinking of having another?
And myself: suddenly sobbing—
I don't want to be pregnant with anyone but Oona.

I don't want to be pregnant with anyone but Oona.

Walking, before you were born

When I walked with myself,
it was you I walked with.
As if something else was carrying me
all the way to I-don't-know-where,
besides my feet.

My daughter brings me a rock and says: *this is your power.*

My daughter brings me a rock and says: *this is your power.*
We run down the cold empty beach, fall
onto a mattress of cool sand.
She gets up—*Can't catch me*—and runs.
Mom, she calls back, *hold onto your power.*
Her nose runs as she runs, on the beach it's only us.
Do you need a tissue? I call out to her . . .
Because . . . eh, I don't have one.

We follow bird tracks and pretend to be birds.
We follow dog tracks and pretend to be dogs.
We draw a broad-shouldered heart in the sand—
jump in and out of its arms.

Can't catch me!
We collapse on our mattress: earth.
Our fingers sift through the particles of rock,
crab-shell, plastic, bone?
With our eyes closed we can't tell the difference.

My daughter hands me a rock and says, *mommy,*
this is your power.
Run with it and you will never lose power.
We   r u n – r u n   n o s e – f a l l   n o s e – r u n.
Do you need a tissue? I call out to her . . .
Because . . . eh, I don't have one.

Sand of shell sand of rock sand of rubber sand of plastic
gunpowder and bone. We can't tell the difference.
With our eyes closed we build sandcastles.
We change earth.
I was just a rock spinning in space.
I didn't know anything could grow on me or for how long.
That she and I are having this conversation is a miracle.

a tethering

Morning Song

little-foot-soles
set the morning
like a breeze. the sound
of shapes willed into being.
pencil-across-paper-sounds
scissors-sounds—
something's being colored in.
(my husband stretches in his mammal-
patterned pajamas,
moos then falls back to sleep.)

my favorite sound
as a child was the *nah-nah-nah*
of my grandparents talking
in the other room as I sleep.
now it's little feet.
you might think it a holiday
by their sound.

little-foot-soles
slap the morning
like a moo.

little-foot-soles under covers
in the triple-hearted-morning,
little-foot-soles for a cuddle with
crumbed feet.

my husband
in his balloon-
patterned pajamas,
(he'd like me to mention he's been working late) stretches
then falls back to sleep.

We lay a blanket on earth for a little picnic

An asteroid with no thought of anything but its own projectile has little concern for its impact—A volcano with good intentions choking air and blocking sun.

I have come to think of earth herself as an astronaut. Her helmet, her bubble of atmosphere. Her tilt toward her sun, her erection—

But I don't know anything—I'm just picnicking here—watching the swish

in the hips of human beings—back and forth and back and forth and back—all the way back to our ancestors the fish.

I don't know anything. Dear Oona,

what if human beings are just tiny volcanoes? What if human beings are just tiny asteroids?

,,
OONADAD

I write WALL on the wall.

I write BATHROOM on the bathroom door and CAT on the wall above the litter bin. I write MIRROR on the mirror so MIRROR appears across our faces.

My three-year-old daughter cackles maniacally. Her joy of letters and language has started a compulsion in the house. I write MOM and DAD on the bedroom door and she draws a picture underneath—That's you on your wedding day.

She draws a picture of herself on her bedroom door and writes her own name. On all the rest of the doors in the house I write DOOR. (Except the hallway closet where she insists on writing a double backwards HI. So: *IH IH.*

I write EARTH and STAR on the wall.

On the refrigerator I write FOOD. BOOK on bookcase. BED on bed. SINK on sink. TUB on tub. On the wall near the toilet my daughter writes HI.

She draws a big rainbow on the hallway wall and I write RAINBOW. She traces the letters with her fingers. She draws a sun on the wall and I write SUN. On the stairs I write STEP.

If you draw a tree on the window, I'll write TREE, I tell her. And we do. If you draw a hippo, I'll write HIPPO, and we do.

She draws a mean caterpillar mommy and a mean caterpillar baby on the wall and I write MEAN CATERPILLAR MOMMY and MEAN CATERPILLAR BABY.

She draws a picture of our family and says—that's you in the lipstick.

I have read some poetry in my life, but the most beautiful sentence I have ever seen in the English language is written by my three-year-old daughter, Oona—in bright pink chalk on the sidewalk in front of my house—

"

OONADAD

OONA and DAD are one word, she explains, because OONA and DAD love you-ch'other. And the two little lines above it? as to offer accent or emphasis? It means they love-you-cho'ther.

A tethering

I can't say what it is to be loved but I think the ingredients are something like my husband sitting by my side as I am diagnosed with gallbladder disease and later that night biting a tit through my T-shirt.

Dear Oona, always be pregnant with something.

a quiet

is the sound of troublemaker
toilet paper
looping around the furniture

as close as food

As Close as Food

I.   Inside my bra are two purple cabbage leaves.

My daughter is six-months-weaned—but my boobs will not stop making milk. Stop, I say, but they don't listen. It's not the first time my body has done something without my permission.

Since I am not feeding, the pressure builds up inside me—a predicament I describe to any sympathetic gentleperson who will listen as being comparable to blue balls.

I am weaning and weeping as I write this—scientists discovered the morsels of an ancient insect on the tip of a fossilized tooth of a 24-million-year-old frog. To be this close—as close as food—I am a lifelong vegetarian—we do not know such closeness.

(Do I smell like cabbage? The enzymes are supposed to bring down the swelling.)

All I did was touch his toes—a friend asked me to hold her infant, just-for-a-minute. What am I supposed to say? Keep your hungry infants away from me? (I said that.) I didn't even hold this child—I just touched his toes and ok, ok—his nose, his nose!

The next morning my breasts were heavy—just under the skin of the nipples porous with white and the milk was near.

It's not the last time my body will do something without my permission—In cafés, at picnic tables, on street corners, at birthday parties my boobs blow up like the balloons of birthday clowns if a baby as much as looks at me or—

I am the village freak—I walk into a local eatery and a friend is dining with a new mother and her infant—It is a business lunch—he introduces me like this—This is Jen, she has a lactation problem. She can't be around babies. I once snuggled with his 8-month-old daughter—for just a minute—as a favor!—and the next morning—a warm bath for my leaking tits!

I can't say much more for fear they are listening—(the boobs)—For fear the slightest suggestion in my mind will cause the milk into production again—The breasts to ache and heavy again—The hormones to build up and bring me to extremes: fatigue, weepiness, restlessness, inability to focus—alternating with the great and maniacal power to feed.

All I can say is—this is proof—Something I am not in control of—is being transmitted—like Wi-Fi—between my body and the bodies of infants—Proof—(a bag of frozen peas for my throbbing tits, please) of Wi-Fi between you and who and who and who

and me.

2. Museum of Natural History, Hall of Evolution

"The Monkey-People have boobs!" you explain
to every hominoid who will listen.
"The Monkey-People have boobs,"
I whisper later as you drink.

The suction breaks,
the sides of the mouth curl up,
and then the holy giggle.

3. The cup

It's not that I'm jealous of water when she drinks it—

It's just the way the cup covers most of her face as she brings it to her lips—the way my boob would cover most of her face before she could speak and she'd sing along with my singing with the wideness of her blueberry eyes—It's the same now—she will have a conversation with only her eyes, or a nod of the head, her face swallowed up mostly by a cup as she drinks—

It's not the water that brings these pangs of envy as much as the flash of an expression from behind the cup.

4. Body, I never knew I could love you

I never loved my body until she was inside it. I never loved my breasts until they made milk for her.

I never understood why people took naked pictures of themselves until she was inside me—The taut and expanding skin over the relentless womb. The anti-gravitational breasts— They are the only naked photos of myself you will find on my computer. Release them I don't care—release them for science.

I'll say it just once and only to myself—I do not want to give up the power to feed my child with my body—

I don't want to give up the power to be able to feed my child without a bowl or grain or utensil or dollar or bottle or government (this government) or job or faucet or jar—and on airplanes!—We are a smooth operating system during takeoffs and landings—passengers come up to me and say your baby could solve world peace—she is the face of the ceasefire.

It scares me to depend completely on the world around us to feed my child. What if we get lost and I forget to pack snacks?—what if the economy dives and we have no money for food?—or a natural disaster?—or the dictator comes to power or some kind of attack?—or?—how will I feed her?

And what about these bouncy tits that knock together when I sex?—I don't want to give them up.

5. The Museum Where They Are Alive

Thank you for this day, mommy.
Thank you for this day, baby.
Do you remember what we did today?
We went to the Museum of Natural History and saw
dinosaurs!
(quiet, dozing off) (then from the quiet . . .)
Mom?
Yes, baby.

For my birthday can we go to the other Museum of Natural
History. And see the alive dinosaurs?
I want you to take me to the museum where they are alive.

6. Shut-up

My boobs speak fluently to babies—shut-up, I tell them, but they don't listen. I live in a perpetual state of engorgement—Sometimes I have the urge to take my just-weaned child in my arms and offer her a nipple—just to clear the tubes. Or just to—?—*Shut-up, shut-up*—be food—

And when she asks—? I pretend I have no milk in me—try to sleep—And the—shut-up—transmit of want between the child and milk in my glands—

I am weaning and weeping as I write this—Scientists have discovered a belly full of squid inside the skeleton of a 200-million-year-old ichthyosaur—What's an ichthyosaur?—It hardly matters with luck like this—

Perhaps we have misunderstood the purpose of our bodies?

If a pet-owner dies alone—the face is usually eaten first. A cheek, some nose—The moral, we tell ourselves, is don't be delicious—And I don't want to die, but being food has changed me. I don't want to die but—Perhaps we have misunderstood.

To eat and be eaten, says Earth, that is life—

Inside a coffin somewhere in Long Island, New York, is my first love—Inside his coffin—*shut-up, shut-up*—is my baseball cap—Inside my baseball cap is his skull—Inside the pelvis of an ancient frog are bits of fish vertebrate—Inside my bra are two enormous cabbage leaves.

wean

a little
less and
a little less and a little

less and then
no more.

but tonight, a little more.

a little
less and
a little less and a little

less and then
no more.

but tonight, a little, a little more.

Opium

When I'm real old, I'll get high on opium all day and dream of what it was like to be food—How it felt when she came out of monkey-me and monkey-she latched on—and gobbled me up—And part of me came out of her monkey ass twenty monkey-minutes later—But!—Next day she was bigger and smarter and part of myself must have carried inside her, must have—I call this "earth syndrome"—This addiction to being life—When I'm old I'll lay back and smoke opium and imagine myself as banana cake or banana tree in an orchard peopled by trees of two hundred million years. And I feed my daughter.

When my daughter learns to use the toilet . . .

We sing to her poops to coax them into this world:

Come out come out come out little poop
And say hello to daughter and me
Come out come out come out little poop
And say hello to mommy and me

My daughter poops a treasure
more valuable to Earth (who eats poop),
than any contribution of the high arts.

Last Meal

Nom-nom-nom—
Mommy, I ate you.
And you died in my tummy.

That would be a nice place to die.

The foot

I lay down next to my child as she sleeps.
Three years ago today she was a ceramicist
molding the elasticity of my skin—
(*A foot!*—A trail inside the sand of me.)
Now, she is more than half the length of my body
as I lay next to her—
untogether and together-still.
She rolls over towards me, heavy with sleep—
The only feeling better than watching her come
towards me
is watching her ditch me
at parties and playgrounds—ditch me
with the sparkle of a college senior.
But right now—in sleep—the foot—
it finds me—kneads
at my stomach
and makes an earth of me.

Thankfool

Oona is at the age where she has mastered phonics but doesn't know the right way to spell so she writes words the way she hears them. "Thankful" as "Thankfool." I know she will eventually have to learn the right way to spell, but how can I go back to "thankful" now that I've seen "thankfool"? I knew I was thankfool the moment I saw it . . . thankfool thankfool thankfool . . . Even as the apparatus I am typing into tries to correct my spelling, I am thankfool . . .

The poems "little astronaut," "An Infant Reaches," and "The Dishes" were performed by Mike Birbiglia in the Broadway production of *The New One* at the Cort Theatre, October 25, 2018–January 20, 2019. Thanks to Mike Birbiglia and Seth Barrish. Several poems from this collection appeared in Mike Birbiglia's *The New One: Painfully True Stories of a Reluctant Dad.* Thanks to Gretchen Young and Grand Central Publishing. "To the Car Seat on My Bathroom Floor" first appeared in the *New York Times* thanks to Jessica Grosse. "Dancing, before you were born" will appear in *Poem-A-Day* and "The Foot" appeared in *Ploughshares.* Thanks to those publications and the Academy of American Poets and Ilya Kaminsky.

My gratitude to the generous life forms *little astronaut* has encountered in her six-year journey: Mike Birbiglia. These poems would be secret poems on my laptop if not for Mike Birbiglia. Rena Mosteirin, who read more versions than anyone, Ilya Kaminsky. People and places that let me perform early versions of poems: The Cherry Lane Theater in New York City, Flanny and Largo at the Coronet in Los Angeles, Paul Muldoon's Picnic at the Irish Arts Center, Judd Apatow, Pete Holmes, The Milk Carton Kids, Sondre Lerche. Moms who grabbed my kid while I finished this book—Jana Duda and Nancy Juvonen—and my own mom. My whole family. Mabel Lewis, Maria Garcia Teutsch, Sarah McEachern, Claire Keane, Paige Lewis, Victoria Labalme, Lewis Black, Derek DelGaudio, Chris Wink, Alan Zweibel, Adam Gopnik, Liz Allen, Jean Hanff Korelitz, John Mulaney, Ira Glass, Chris Crawford, Bella Lewis, and Bill Roberts. My cat, Mazzy Star Macaroni. My amazing editor, Allison Adler, and everyone at Andrews McMeel for making this book better and putting it into the world. The heroic Erin Malone who made this book possible. I am thankfool to all.

little astronaut is for Moe & O.

little astronaut

Andrews McMeel Publishing
a division of Andrews McMeel Universal
1130 Walnut Street, Kansas City, Missouri 64106

www.andrewsmcmeel.com

17 18 19 20 21 VEP 10 9 8 7 6 5 4 3 2 1

ISBN: 9781524872205

Library of Congress Control Number: 2021949169

Editor: Allison Adler
Art Director: Julie Barnes
Production Editor: Brianna Westervelt
Production Manager: Carol Coe

Illustration by Joy Hwang Ruiz

ATTENTION: SCHOOLS AND BUSINESSES
Andrews McMeel books are available at quantity discounts with
bulk purchase for educational, business, or sales promotional use.
For information, please e-mail the Andrews McMeel Publishing
Special Sales Department: specialsales@amuniversal.com.